# A SLIM VOLUME

*Glyndebourne:
an anecdotal account*

George Christie

George Christie
wryly referred to his book as
a 'slim volume'.
He would have delved further
into more memories of
Glyndebourne,
but ran out of life.
This, as he said, is
'for the record'.

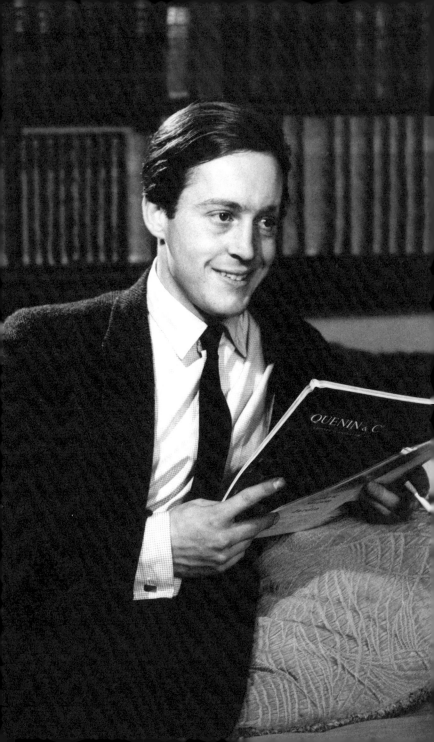

# INTRODUCTION

*Louise Flind pays tribute to her father,*
*George Christie*

A t a Sunday lunch in November 2013, Mum whispered as she came through the door 'He's going to write the book'. After years of buttoning his lip, selectively, it was time to unbutton abundantly. Latterly he would delight visitors to Old House, the beautiful farmhouse where he and Mum moved to from Glyndebourne, with outrageous and charming indiscretions. This book isn't an extension of those, more an anecdotal sequel to Spike Hughes's *Glyndebourne, A History of the Festival Opera*. I naively hoped that writing this book might give him a new lease of life.

Once the decision had been made, there was no stopping him. With jugular determination, and perhaps a brave understanding that time was running out, he put pen to paper in the kitchen at Old House. This jeopardised lunch, Mum's favourite meal, so he was moved upstairs to his dressing room. He had an extremely nice office in a barn but it was freezing and there was no question of putting on the heating. I went to have lunch with him one day when Mum was out and he was at his kitchen desk. I was met at the door by Fred, the pug, and in the kitchen by his raised hand. After five minutes of writing he said 'OK'. He wrote the book almost entirely from memory and pretty accurate it is. He prided himself on a rather good memory which made arguments all the more enjoyable for him.

In March 2014 he took a punt and booked himself into the Harley Street Clinic for pioneering heart surgery. It didn't come off, his wretched body failed him and he returned home frail and downbeat. He had taken the book to Harley Street in his briefcase. Also packed in the briefcase was a little snifter which he managed to spill out on some of the pages – he was distraught about this, and at the loss of the drink, but marginally cheered up when I took him in a tin of vodka and tonic, only to be caught by a nurse sipping it while tethered to a dialysis machine. A spell in the Sussex County Hospital with a sea view restored his spirits but not his little body.

Glyndebourne was Dad, and Dad was Glyndebourne, but neither was either without Mum. They married in 1958 when she was 21 and he 23.

My eldest brother Hector was born in 1961, John Christie, Dad's father, died in 1962 and Glyndebourne became their life. Neither Mum nor Dad thought of it as work, but more a way of life, which they adored, hated, resented and loved. Because of this, they maintained the ethos of the place, which had really been initialised by my grandmother, Audrey Mildmay. The house, although a family home, houses directors, music staff, conductors and choreographers throughout the Festival and touring periods. Being cut off geographically makes for a hugger-mugger company which, to some extent, suits a theatre. Dad was vigorous in providing the best conditions to work in. As he latterly jotted down: 'A happy work force makes for a happy company makes for a happy audience'. Many of those he and Mum worked with became firm friends. His greatest fascination was the intricacies of putting a production on stage – from the idea, to booking the conductor, director and designer, the casting, the model showing, the scenery, the props and costumes, and he would follow their progress intently. But it wasn't just the artists who became friends. At one company Christmas lunch he leant over to the table beside him inhabited by the transport drivers and chided 'Drink up, transport'.

John Christie loved the Germans because they didn't bomb Glyndebourne in the war – he probably felt the place had held its own. Similarly Dad loved Glyndebourne for its individuality and non-institutionalism, something which he and Mum strove to protect, whilst determinedly keeping the place up-to-date.

Ultimately Dad was resolutely proud of Gus, my brother, once he realised and accepted that he was a different beast from himself. While Dad would pore and tinker over his last-night speech, need a beta blocker and the odd sip of Retsina, Gus writes it on the afternoon of the last night and strides onto the stage as if he's getting on a tube train – different beasts – and they increasingly recognised the qualities in one another as time went by. In 2005 Gus asked me to be on the Board. I was delighted, then aghast when I realised I had taken Dad's place. He didn't want to hover and retreated to Old House to grumble, and I don't think he ever regretted this decision.

On one of my last visits to Dad, I spotted Barry, their part-time gardener, out of the window with his shirt off. 'He's a good lad, Barry', said Dad, 'but he hasn't got the height of that hedge right. It needs to be lower so you can see the view, but your mother disagrees. Keep an eye on that hedge, would you?' He prided himself on his attention to detail and often advised us to 'get a grip' on all things. By the spring of that year it was obvious that the end was approaching and that he had had enough of life. He chose to be at home and take a grip on death with the same blend of strength, charm and determination that he had shown throughout his life.

*Louise Flind*
*December 2015*

# PREFACE

My father never wrote an autobiography – a story which would have highlighted innovation, daring, achievement and, as it turned out, startling success.

There seems to me to be three reasons for writing a book in which you take centre stage – you have enough to say to entice a wide readership and therefore the prospect of beguiling royalties; you have excessive self-esteem; or you want to set the record straight, before somebody else distorts the truth.

My father couldn't have cared a fig. I have had similar feelings, but aged 79 I have awoken with a jolt to the extent of the escalation of the media's and the general public's misinterpretation of Glyndebourne: where and what it stands for and what it has achieved.

My father was given to mission statements – a risky business given that such statements tend to be a rather crude form of PR, bombast or just plain bullshit.

Added to this is the risk of failing to meet all the objectives set out in the mission statement. However, he was highly individualistic and possessed a considerable degree of eccentricity which often softened the blast of his statements, but caused my mother, whose feet were firmly on the ground, to get into a pickle of apprehension. They were in a constant state of battle: the realisation of his visionary ideas and his self-belief versus her practicality and well-grounded understanding of the adventurous path their lives were set to pursue.

I am more of a wilting violet, preferring understatement on the subject of aims and aspirations.

It is therefore odd that I should take it upon myself to write a book which is intended to be an anecdotal account – not a biography – of Glyndebourne, whilst my Dad never formally got round to putting pen to paper about his ground-breaking achievements.

A variety of books on Glyndebourne have been published over the years – notably Spike Hughes's *Glyndebourne: A History of the Festival Opera 1934-64*, which he subsequently extended in synoptic form to 1980. However, his is the only officially commissioned story in authoritative form and concludes in 1980.

So a recollection of the achievements of my parents and observations of what followed during my time as Chairman might perhaps not be out of place.

# PRE-WAR FOUNDATIONS

The birth of 'country-house opera' as it is now generically – and rather disparagingly – known, was launched at Glyndebourne in 1934. It was inspired by my parents who had the extraordinary good fortune to nobble Fritz Busch and Carl Ebert who, although not Jewish, were refugees from Hitler's increasingly repressive regime. All of this is well-documented, but justifies brief repetition in the context of the burgeoning growth and spread of 'country-house opera'. Glyndebourne was conceived by a team of talent, experience and international reputation, which gave it a head start and pitched it immediately into the 'first league'. Glyndebourne was starting half-way up the hill of its aspiration.

My father was unconsciously following in the footsteps of a tradition prevalent in earlier centuries when the playground of opera was provided in the courts of European aristocrats. 'Country-house opera' is not quite the preserve of the 20th century it is now popularly made out to be – the main difference between now and, say, the 18th century, is that the audience pay for their predilection.

My father was by nature practical and resourceful, hence the reality of his achievement, but idealism with all its pitfalls was given equal opportunity in his scheme of objectives. Hence the mission statements.

He fitted no conventional models. The family owned several quite large estates in Sussex, Devon and Lincolnshire. He inherited the Sussex and Devon properties, and was not interested in ownership *per se* but in turning his assets to good account – be it for commercial profit or social/charitable gain. He was born in 1882 and was inevitably steeped in the mores of Victorian culture which conventionally fitted his birthright. He was by his up-bringing a conservative, but he was politically an odd-ball unaffiliated to any political party whilst holding steadfastly to what he believed was the right way forward in society. He was an eccentric – Childs, his butler, was his Best Man – and my godfather. Not positions customarily taken up by butlers. But Childs was an exception to the rule and must be the only butler ever to get an obituary in *The Times*.

Whilst my father was innately practical he was also prone to unrealistic ideas that were on the whole emotionally rather than intellectually motivated, and it was in this context that my mother's influence came valuably into play. With her background as a professional singer she brought ballast to the balloons of fancy which he concocted. She was also invaluable in providing the heartbeat which was a hallmark in Glyndebourne's nascent years and which, I like to think, my wife and I perpetuated with fervour later on.

In the years leading up to the war Glyndebourne concentrated largely on the works of Mozart: the three da Ponte operas, *Die Zauberflöte* and *Die Entführung aus dem Serail* – Donizetti's *Don Pasquale* and Verdi's *Macbeth* (its UK premiere) were added to the repertoire in 1938 and 1939. Ebert directed everything and Busch conducted most of the performances. My father liked to aim high and he asked Arturo Toscanini to consider conducting an opera at Glyndebourne to which Toscanini replied: 'But you're already blessed with Busch'. Perhaps the most self-deprecatory remark he ever made.

Opera directors at the time were a rare breed in the UK and received no acknowledgement on playbills or in programmes as the dramatic content of opera was largely neglected. Ebert, with Busch's connivance, corrected this situation emphatically, providing Glyndebourne's performances with a rational balance – the dramatic narrative being given equal weight through the expression of music. The marriage of these ingredients is, after all, fundamental to the performance of opera – until, that is, the individuals get out of kilter and, as is wont to happen nowadays, the dramatic content is wantonly distorted.

Starting an opera company from scratch without public subsidy is a fairly lunatic concept and needs passion. Of the recent growth of companies that have sprung up, it seems to me that Garsington – a one-man band under the late Leonard Ingrams – takes the biscuit simply because he had very considerable knowledge of the operatic repertoire and an unswerving passion for it. Longborough, with its founders, Martin and Lizzie Graham, and Music Director, Anthony Negus, possesses an abundance of similar attributes. However, once set up, an opera company's continuation will depend to a major extent on the choice of principal conductors and leading stage directors. This is where Glyndebourne scored perhaps above all others. Busch and Ebert had international reputations and they in turn attracted singers off the 'top shelf' – such as Willi Domgraf-Fassbänder, Dino Borgioli, Salvatore Baccaloni, Luise Helletsgruber, Alexander Kipnis, Aulikki Rautawaara, Ina Souez, Mariano Stabile and Risë Stevens. These singers are now almost forgotten – mainly because recordings of opera which help to maintain a singer's reputation were in scarce supply at that time. Busch and Ebert also brought their power of persuasion into play in engaging Rudolf Bing as General Manager – a real coup for

Glyndebourne, as he was one of the most outstanding entrepreneurs in the operatic world at the time.

The alchemy of the Busch, Ebert and Bing mixture combined with the feed-in from my parents gave Glyndebourne a kick-start which has had lasting effect.

My father fought in the First World War but at the age of 58 was not of course called up for the Second. So he spent a certain amount of time proposing grandiose ideas as to how to set the world to rights and, in particular, to bring some logic to the traditional chaos of opera in this country, culminating in his bid to buy the Royal Opera House, Covent Garden. My mother had taken my sister and me to North America during the war and so was unable to hold my father's flights of fancy in check. He was, thank heavens, pipped at the post in his quest to buy Covent Garden by John Maynard Keynes who negotiated its purchase for the nation.

Imagine now being the owner/manager of Glyndebourne *and* the owner/manager of the ROH. Talk about biting off more than you can chew. My gratitude to Keynes is boundless.

# POST-WAR BUILDING BLOCKS

In 1946 and 1947 Glyndebourne and Benjamin Britten found themselves in courtship with the world premieres of *The Rape of Lucretia* (1946) and *Albert Herring* (English Opera Group, 1947). It soon became abundantly clear that a fully consummated marriage was not on the cards. Ben and my father could not have been more ill-assorted in virtually every aspect of life and a rumpus between the two ensued, culminating with total estrangement on each side – sad but inevitable. Following the run of performances of these two productions, Glyndebourne, also in 1947, mounted Gluck's *Orfeo ed Euridice*, with Kathleen Ferrier performing the role of Orfeo for the first time in a production staged by Ebert who, like Busch, had played no part in the two Britten operas.

My father at this point faced the major challenge of how to continue funding his enterprise at Glyndebourne. Up to this moment he had taken it upon himself to build his opera house at his own expense and to give each Festival the financial support it required. He hit upon the idea of passing the buck to somebody else, and it was my mother who championed Edinburgh as the best equipped to take on this burden. Rudi Bing cajoled the City Fathers there and in particular the Provost, Sir John Falconer, to carry this idea forward to fruition – with Bing in charge of the content from planning to materialisation. All this was done from our London offices in Baker Street and the administrative staff then moved up to Edinburgh three weeks before the opening night. The Edinburgh Festival provided a showcase which, because there weren't any other showcases in Europe, captured many of the greatest musicians, such as the pianist Artur Schnabel, the cellist Pierre Fournier and the conductor Bruno Walter. Glyndebourne was very much the axis of the Festival around which these brilliant artists set their stall. Heady days.

Glyndebourne administered the Edinburgh Festival from 1947 to 1949 inclusive, when Bing resigned his position as General Manager of Glyndebourne and Edinburgh to go to the Metropolitan Opera in New York. His 'sidekicks', Moran Caplat and Ian Hunter, succeeded him at Glyndebourne and Edinburgh respectively.

Glyndebourne in Sussex went 'dark' in these three years, but it put its toe in the spa waters of Bath, where it mounted a festival in 1948. However, my father and Bing found the local response there 'dozy' and so for Glyndebourne that was the end of that venture, although Glyndebourne could perhaps claim responsibility for giving birth – albeit a semi-comatose birth – to the Bath Festival.

My father then found a backer, John Spedan Lewis (who to a large extent had created a 'co-operative' in the shops of the John Lewis Partnership), and 1950 saw the re-opening of the Festival in Sussex. We continued to perform also in Edinburgh for five of the next six years. The many summer holidays from school I spent in that city have given me an abiding love for it, and I regard it as a contestant for pride of place in the top five most beautiful cities in the world.

In 1951 the Glyndebourne Festival received state subsidy for the first and last time – as part of the Festival of Britain on which Clement Attlee's government blew a lot of money (creating most famously the Southbank Centre). I tried some 15 years later to get subsidy from the Arts Council (originally called the Council for the Encouragement of Music and the Arts (CEMA) – translated by my father as the Council for the Encouragement of the Mediocre Arts) and had a meeting with Arnold Goodman, Chairman of the Council, and George Harewood, Chairman of the Council's Music Panel, at which I outlined the case for subsidy for the Festival. Goodman argued that this would be regarded as subsidy for Glyndebourne's wealthy audience. I countered this by suggesting that with Arts Council support I could lower the price of the tickets. He responded to this by saying in that event the additional subsidy per seat sold would provide total support to Glyndebourne out of all proportion to that given to the Council's other 'clients'. I went away with my tail between my legs – and have been indebted to Goodman and Harewood ever since, treasuring Glyndebourne's independence.

At this point in the early 1950s further financial reinforcement arrived on the scene in the shape of Nicholas (Miki) Sekers, a Hungarian with a very thick accent which belied his nationality. Sekers had settled in Cumbria in 1937 where there was a drive to bring new industry to the economically-depressed area of West Cumberland. Sekers, whose family business was in textiles, was keen to start a similar business in England, so he set about picking a suitable site and then building his silk mills. With a few skilled textile workers from Hungary, he trained a group of local ladies how to operate the 50 or so looms in his factory and thus gave birth in 1938 to the West Cumberland Silk Mills – turning out, as it happens, a valuable source of silk for the manufacture of parachutes during the war. Miki was exotic in character and in lifestyle – and bursting with ideas. He rather surprisingly befriended my father and mother and introduced the idea of the Festival's Programme Book, more or less as we now know it, which provided an income stream from the sale of pages of advertisements. Building on this financial success he encouraged my parents to set up the Glyndebourne Festival Society (effectively a form of 'Friends of Glyndebourne') to provide a revenue stream from subscriptions. On top of this he provided the costume material for a variety of productions – Oliver Messel's designs making the greatest demands on Miki's generosity.

As Glyndebourne became more commercial in its quest for financial independence and stability, it also toyed with the idea of obtaining charitable status. At the time such status had not been granted to any performing arts organisation – and wasn't sought. However, my father became increasingly convinced that as a registered charity he would be released in some degree from the financial burden falling almost exclusively on him. My mother, on the other hand, had forebodings that the family's power-base would be threatened. She was somehow won over (or trampled on), and so it was that the Glyndebourne Arts Trust was born with an eminent bunch of trustees. It took more than a year and a half to persuade the Charity Commission to make this concession and entailed top-level legal debate. Glyndebourne was the first arts organisation to be registered as a charity – and the Charity Commission's doors were then stormed by everyone involved in the arts seeking the same treatment.

In the 1930s Glyndebourne had started a

fruitful relationship with the BBC transmitting radio broadcasts from the theatre. It extended this relationship in 1951 by leading the way with the first live television transmission of a complete opera, *Così fan tutte*. This collaboration between Glyndebourne and the BBC resulted in the broadcast of several operas in succeeding years and placed Glyndebourne as the leader of all opera companies in this line of business – a curious situation given its very limited number of productions each year on which the BBC could feed. In 1960 Glyndebourne joined forces again with the BBC when, for the first time, an opera (*Don Giovanni*) was performed at the Proms – since when Glyndebourne has featured there every year. Television and the Proms broadened Glyndebourne's audience exposure to a valuable extent at the time when its limited Festival output was threatened by criticism of pandering exclusively to a wealthy elite.

The 16 post-war years up to my father's death in 1962 saw the resignation of Bing in 1949 and the demise of Busch in 1951 and my mother in 1953, together with the retirement of Ebert in 1959 – effectively a clean sweep of all those who can be credited for their vision, their passion and determination, and for the assortment of their professional skills which created and nurtured Glyndebourne. The building blocks they instituted have been unshakeable.

# TRANSITION

In 1948 Vittorio Gui conducted *Così fan tutte* and in 1949 Verdi's *Un ballo in maschera*. Busch returned in 1950 for a couple of productions, and for all six productions in 1951 – with some assistance from John Pritchard, a rising star at that time. Following Busch's death in 1951, Gui effectively took over as Glyndebourne's Chief Conductor and shared his responsibilities with John Pritchard in a junior role.

In the first 19 years of Glyndebourne's existence Busch had focussed to a large extent on the operas of Mozart, whose works then were not acknowledged with the high regard in which they are now held. Gui (an excellent Mozartian), on the other hand, brought Rossini's operas – relatively neglected at the time (except of course for *Il barbiere di Siviglia*) – to the fore, starting with *La Cenerentola* (a rarity then), followed by *Il barbiere* and then by *Le Comte Ory* (another rarity). Gui, like Busch, never stood between the audience and the composer. It was as if he had a divine line of contact with the composer and at the same time direct empathy with his singers. There were occasions in mid-performance when he would lay his baton down, turn to the audience and grin with satisfaction – letting the composer speak for himself and giving his singers full rein. With singers like Sesto Bruscantini, Juan Oncina, Graziella Sciutti and Tereza Berganza he could afford to do this with beneficial results. Gui was hugely benign. Once there was a power-cut during the start of the dungeon scene in *Fidelio* resulting, of course, in total darkness. Richard Lewis and the orchestra continued to perform 'in step' to the end of Florestan's aria. Gui had laid his baton down and on the reinstatement of the lighting was clearly put out by his apparent dispensability in circumstances which he had not concocted. His benignity was challenged. For me, Gui was the greatest exponent of Rossini's music – it was never driven as is so often the case – and a very great conductor of copious sensitivity embracing a wide variety of repertory. Throughout the 1950s and early 1960s he was, in all but title, Busch's successor.

Mention must be made here that in the mid-1950s Glyndebourne engaged Carlo Maria Giulini and Georg Solti in their operatic debuts in this country, conducting *Falstaff* and *Don Giovanni* respectively – pretty swanky. But sadly their tangle with Glyndebourne was fleeting. Gui felt his position of power was threatened by Giulini, and Solti (who was a misfit at Glyndebourne) was then the perfect 'fit' at

Covent Garden. Ebert, Messel and Gui made a formidable trio in the case of the Rossini operas, and their *Figaro* saw off all competition. Messel triumphantly represented the end of an era, providing designs of great beauty painted on canvas. Scenery constructed in much more durable material (and a nightmare to store) was round the corner. The last productions Glyndebourne staged in sets draped in painted canvas were Hockney's *Die Zauberflöte* and *The Rake's Progress* in the 1970s – the latter, in particular, a victorious anachronism.

The supremo who pulled all the strings in the administration of Glyndebourne's activities was Moran Caplat, a sub-mariner in the war, who survived a torpedo attack and was a prisoner of war in Italy. Then, as Bing's associate at Glyndebourne, he learnt the 'ropes' of opera, having had ambitions before the war to be an actor. He very quickly had a commanding grasp of the job, most of which he had to learn 'on the hoof'. He had an alert mind and he could complete *The Times* crossword on the train between Haywards Heath and Victoria. He cultivated productive relationships with Busch and Ebert and then with Gui, all of whom, fortuitously for Caplat, had rigorous devotion to Glyndebourne – and he built up an excellent team of specialist heads of department. My father was at this point ageing and delegating more and more responsibility, most of which fell on Caplat's shoulders and Caplat incontestably became captain of the ship. The depth of his knowledge of opera was quite shallow in his early years, but he had the good fortune to have the help and guidance of Jani Strasser who had been appointed head of Glyndebourne's music staff. A highly individualistic Hungarian who had started his association with Glyndebourne even before a trench was dug or a brick laid, Strasser was my mother's singing teacher in Vienna in the early 1930s. He was steeped in the knowledge of opera and what was going on in most of the European opera houses. He commanded huge respect from the singers and in the early process of music rehearsals acted as a valuable liaison between conductors and singers and sometimes, he would think, between composers long dead and the singers. As time went on his influence on artistic policy became more pervasive and there was a risk on occasions of discontent between Caplat and Strasser. It was at this point in the 1960s that I, as Chairman, should have taken more of a grip, but I was a callow, inexperienced and self-effacing youth led by, rather than leading, these two well-honed operators. In the course of time I like to think that I managed in some degree to correct this situation.

My father died in 1962. He was given quite a send-off with a memorial service to a packed congregation in Westminster Abbey. Quentin Hailsham (an old friend) gave the address and Mozart's *Requiem* was performed by Glyndebourne artists. It was a moving occasion befitting the celebration of one of

Britain's most pioneering figureheads in the world of opera. It left me as Chairman in name only. I had been working for the previous five years as an assistant to the director of the Gulbenkian Foundation, helping to formulate a policy to bring greater financial support to the arts in the UK, without duplication of the support already supplied, and then, for a time, implementing this policy. This brought me into touch with a good many leading lights in the broad spectrum of the arts. It also gave me an artificial position of power – with the likes of Laurence Olivier begging me for money – and gave my confidence a nudge which it badly needed. As Chairman of Glyndebourne, however, the roles were reversed and I found myself in the position of begging for money.

In 1959 Ebert retired as Artistic Director, although he continued to direct operas until 1963. He directed some 26 productions and brought the function of the director successfully into line with that of the conductor. At the start of his commitment to Glyndebourne he was, of his time, undeniably one of the great, if not the greatest, international stage directors. His last two new productions at Glyndebourne – Strauss's *Der Rosenkavalier* with Régine Crespin, Elisabeth Söderström and Anneliese Rothenberger (an unsurpassable trio); and a divine *Pelléas et Mélisande* (Debussy) with Denise Duval in the eponymous female role – were testimony to his talent. Duval had made her debut with the Glyndebourne company in 1960 as Poulenc's *La Voix humaine*. At a certain point in rehearsals she remonstrated with Jean Cocteau, the director, and also the librettist, pleading for a prompter as a 'safety net', given that she was on-stage for 45 minutes and anxious that she would have difficulty getting back on track should she have a lapse of memory. A member of the music staff had the presence of mind to step in to her rescue by reminding her that most of her performance was on the telephone and in the event that she 'dried' he was always at the other end of the line.

In 1960 Günther Rennert, a big cheese in Germany, was already set on course to assume Ebert's position having staged Beethoven's *Fidelio*, with Gré Brouwenstjin as Leonore and Gui conducting to the manner (or rather the manner of Beethoven) born, and *Don Giovanni*. Rennert was a force to be reckoned with, and his ten-year stint at Glyndebourne was characterised by a lot of choppy water. In 1962 he directed with acclaim Monteverdi's *L'incoronazione di Poppea* in Raymond Leppard's version – a major breakthrough by Glyndebourne in starting to dust down the Baroque repertoire and bringing it to life for a 20th-century audience. Rennert extended this breakthrough in 1967 when he staged Cavalli's *L'Ormindo* with Leppard conducting.

In the early 1960s Franco Enriquez had looked as if he might in the course of time become a contestant as Ebert's successor. Enriquez was the stepson of Gui and made his first UK appearance in

1952 when, at the age of 25, he directed Bellini's *Norma* at Covent Garden, with Gui conducting and Callas (who adored him) making her debut there in the title role. In 1960 Enriquez, an extraordinarily beguiling individual, first directed at Glyndebourne, Bellini's *I puritani* starring Joan Sutherland. He then went on to direct *Die Zauberflöte* in an ingeniously conceived production with beautiful designs by Emanuele Luzzati. However, Enriquez was becoming increasingly unreliable and in 1970 a production of Rossini's *Il turco in Italia*, which had been offered to him (he then defected late in the day) was instead diverted to John Cox – the start of a long and productive liaison.

John Cox, who had been an assistant director at Glyndebourne since 1959, directed 17 productions between 1970 and 1984. He was appointed Director of Productions in 1972 and the highlights of his tenure which stick in the memory are Strauss's *Capriccio* in 1973, with Söderström, and later Felicity Lott, performing the role of the Countess; *Intermezzo* in 1975, again with Söderström taking a central role; and Stravinsky's *The Rake's Progress* in the same year in Hockney's sets. The Strauss productions set the seal on a revival of interest in his comedies. *Ariadne auf Naxos* was previously the only one which was performed universally, an opera which Cox directed at Glyndebourne in 1971. He took Sweden's enchanting theatre in Drottningholm as the spring-board for Michael Annals's designs of Strauss's masterpiece, the *Ariadne* Prologue. *Capriccio* was (like

*Rosenkavalier*) located by Strauss and his librettist (Clemens Krauss) in the 18th century. Cox decided to shed all the crinolines and bring the narrative into an era the audience might relate to, namely the early 1920s when the vestiges of stilted conversation still held sway in the salons of London and Paris. I remonstrated with Cox about updating the opera, pointing out the anachronism of La Roche's remark in the libretto to the effect that he had a date to meet Goldoni (the 18th-century playwright). Cox leafed through a London telephone directory and pointed out a list of Goldonis. His production of *Capriccio* was a triumph and has travelled world-wide. His later production of *Intermezzo* in designs by Martin Battersby (who carried out the updated and specially apt redecoration of the *Capriccio* sets) was similarly triumphant and won the *Evening Standard Award*. These two operas had little currency value outside Vienna and Munich until Cox gave them his treatment.

Then along came Cox's *Rake* in 1975 – popularly known as 'Hockney's *Rake*'. It was very much Cox's idea to engage David Hockney to create the designs for this opera, and it was above all Cox who determined how the designs would illustrate and help to unfold the narrative; it was Hockney who inimitably brought all this to reality. The production should in all conscience carry the soubriquet as 'Cox and Hockney's *Rake*'. This is not intended to detract anything from Hockney's achievement (I have huge admiration for him), but it is intended to set the record straight. It was a joint and joyous (if dramatically sad) venture and, like *Capriccio*, continues to be replicated world-wide.

Through three decades culminating in the late 1970s the flow of John Pritchard's input was extensive. He started at Glyndebourne as Busch's assistant and very soon found himself conducting operas which Busch, through ill-health, was unable to do. Pritchard had innate talent: he had an immediate grasp of a full score of any complexity or of any composer, whatever the era – ancient or modern. Because he had such a facility he laboured under a yoke of indolence. He was a hedonist and indulged in the best things in life. As a result he was not taken as seriously as his extraordinary talent merited, but on form he was unsurpassable. I remember when he took over *Die Entführung aus dem Serail* from Zubin Mehta in Salzburg (a famous production by Georgio Strehler) and conjured up a sublime performance and, on several occasions, at Glyndebourne where although for one reason or another he had had little rehearsal he did likewise. On the rare occasions when he was off-form he was inevitably routine.

Pritchard never had an affiliation with any of the recording companies and so memory of his achievements would be short-lived. He worked in almost all of the major opera houses, but Glyndebourne was essentially central to his life. He conducted at Glyndebourne for 26 consecutive years from 1951 to 1977, encompassing with equal ease the diverse repertoire of 14 composers – a valuable and indispensable ingredient in Glyndebourne's post-war development.

So far I have concentrated largely on directors and conductors who, in key positions, guided Glyndebourne's development up to the end of the 1970s. Up to the early 1960s Glyndebourne was in the safe and creative hands of my father and mother and of Busch, Ebert and Gui. Then the powerful influence of these individuals dwindled largely through death. For the latter part of the 1960s Glyndebourne experienced a number of troughs interspersed with a diminishing volume of peaks.

Caplat's eventful hold on the administration of the company was becoming wayward and Strasser's grip on the workings of the music department was over-reaching itself. There was a general uncertainty about Glyndebourne's artistic policy and its social responsibilities. It simply lacked the leadership which the old brigade had brought to it and I was inexperienced. However, steps were taken to get Glyndebourne back on a progressive course, starting with the creation of Glyndebourne Touring Opera in 1968, and the introduction of new artistic leadership at the start of the 1970s.

39

# RESUSCITATION

The media have always made a bit of a thing about Glyndebourne's bucolic setting characterised by extravagant picnics on the lawns and the popping of champagne corks – posh gluttony jockeying for precedence over the performance of opera. With the burgeoning growth of 'country house opera' and its attendant picnics, this is now largely taken for granted and takes up fewer column inches in the press. However, one basic factor which seems to escape the media's understanding of the position has to do with the tradition of picnicking and with the lack of restaurant accommodation to house the entire audience – and the last thing I want to do is increase the amount of built structure. Generous provision is made to house and cater for the audience, and any additional accommodation would do nothing for the place and would be uneconomical. So that's that and we will continue to be socially divisive in the eyes of some of the press. (Incidentally, I hate the discomfort of picnics and I don't like champagne.)

Glyndebourne's elitism is something which has always exercised my mind. Our exposure through commercial recordings, on television and radio transmissions, and at the Proms, brought my conscience some comfort, but there was a need to extend this exposure and this gave rise to the idea of creating a touring company. Elitism, incidentally, has considerable commercial value, but ideally should run alongside initiatives which aspire to broaden accessibility.

The key objectives for the creation of Glyndebourne Touring Opera were to take Glyndebourne's productions to a wider audience than could be reached within the confines of Glyndebourne, to do this at 'affordable' box office prices and to exploit young British talent. We have always in my memory coached casts of understudies for every soloist in all our Festival productions – as insurance cover. Much of this well-prepared talent, although in most cases not having been called on to perform at Glyndebourne, was then picked up and exploited by other companies.

I approached the Arts Council to provide subsidy which would help to meet our costs and off-set our reduced income from the box office. They responded with an offer of a pitiable amount. I refused it and told them I would be reapplying the next year. I then persuaded the Gulbenkian

Foundation to provide support on a tapered basis over three years (1968-1970). The Arts Council, seeing the increased viability of the project, agreed to provide the subsidy we needed.

The choice of venues toured by GTO was in large measure determined by the Arts Council, who were, and are, responsible for the logical pattern of operatic provision and fair distribution of the money to back it. We tried in some venues to build up a strong affiliation which made economic sense, but which in most cases was relatively short-lived because the pattern of the touring circuit was forever changing. In 1968 our principal competitors were Sadler's Wells (now English National Opera), Opera For All, Welsh National Opera and Scottish Opera. Opera North was created later as an off-shoot of English National Opera to give greater justification for the support they received in London alone, and this added materially to the contest fought for certain venues. GTO has for a long time been an integral part of Glyndebourne's output.

There were two occasions during the first 20 years of GTO's history when the Arts Council seriously threatened to withdraw its support. We fought a fierce and persuasively reasoned campaign on each occasion. At one point I suggested that we might instead of our touring opera, mount mini-festivals of commissioned operas, renewal of repertory seeming to me to be a priority in the future of the art form. The Council responded to this by stating a preference for us to continue our annual tours. Viva GTO.

GTO was, I think I can claim, my brain-child but it was Brian Dickie who largely turned it into reality and nurtured its development. Dickie, on leaving Trinity College, Dublin, took on a lowly job working as Strasser's 'dogsbody'. There are few people from whom you could learn more about the inner workings of opera than Jani Strasser. Dickie's passion for the art form and his administrative ability soon gained him recognition and, with enthusiastic backing from me among others, he was appointed as the Administrator of GTO which flourished under him with box office takings often exceeding those earned by its competitors. He was by this time already Caplat's second mate.

Sir Alfred Beit, Chairman of the Wexford Festival, telephoned me one day and told me that Walter Legge had agreed to succeed Tom Walsh, the founder of the Festival and its Chief Executive, but because of ill health had had to renounce the offer. Did I know, asked Sir Alfred, of anyone who might replace Legge? In those days GTO operated in the spring, and Wexford is an autumn festival. So I was quick to suggest Dickie who could then broaden his knowledge, especially of the international market for singers on whom Wexford depended. Dickie ran the Wexford Festival – with considerable acclaim and informed imagination – until 1971. In that year Glyndebourne swapped its operation to the autumn, thereby clashing with the Wexford Festival. He played his cards with considerable diplomacy and in the process assumed control over a wide variety of administrative functions – particularly and increasingly in the area of casting singers – and continued the task of managing GTO whilst reinforcing Caplat's administration of the Festival. Eventually in 1982 he succeeded Caplat as General Administrator. His management and policies brimmed with determination and invention. He was, for example, responsible for the production of Gershwin's *Porgy and Bess* with Simon Rattle and Trevor Nunn, and for the engagement of the director Nikolaus Lehnhoff and the designer Tobias Hoheisel for the visionary series of Janáček's operas.

Dickie is a pre-eminent impresario in the world of opera – imaginative in the exploitation of a mix of repertoire, an influential and very well informed judge of singing talent and he possesses a real grasp of the financial management of an opera company. He should, after his successful tenure at Glyndebourne, have been seriously considered for the key position at the Royal Opera House or the Met.

It was in the late 1960s that Glyndebourne chanced upon an intriguing proposition. Peter Hall attended a performance of Tchaikovsky's *Eugene Onegin* with Söderström – an unsurpassable Tatyana – and after this performance told me he was leaving the Royal Shakespeare Company. He wanted to concentrate on making films and also on opera which would provide him with a dimension unattainable in the straight theatre. He craved this and Glyndebourne seemed to be the perfect fit for him in this scheme of things. Caplat and the Board of Directors backed the idea with enthusiasm, and a letter was dispatched to Hall outlining what his contractual responsibilities would be at Glyndebourne. Some six months later, Hall sent me a telegram saying that his first two films had not worked out and that the Royal Opera House had offered him a contract. Despondency about this turn of events, however, was allayed shortly afterwards when he became disenchanted with the way things were turning out at the Royal Opera House and he would not after all join Colin Davis and John Tooley there. Instead, much to the chagrin of the Royal Opera House, he agreed to direct Cavalli's *La Calisto* at Glyndebourne in 1970 with Leppard conducting and a cast led by Ileana Cotrubas and Janet Baker – the hottest ticket in opera that summer. It was designed by John Bury to perfection in a production which was 18th century in conception, but ingeniously 20th century in execution. This, of course, was the start of a long, happy and productive association with Hall –

during which time he also became very actively involved as the Artistic Director (1973-1988) at the National Theatre. Max Rayne, the Chairman of the National Theatre, was not infrequently on the telephone asking me for Hall's whereabouts. (Labour strikes were very much in fashion at the time and Chief Executives were therefore expected to be constantly at the helm. No wonder Rayne was so anxious to pin Hall down.) Two years later, in 1972, Hall staged Monteverdi's *Il ritorno d'Ulisse in patria*, again with Baker in a lead role and again in 18th-century designs by Bury using 20th-century technology. All the gods were on aerial tracks and the show was deftly dubbed 'Monteverdi's Flying Circus' by Anne Howells who was playing the Goddess Minerva. This finally put the stamp on Glyndebourne as the revivalist which pumped blood through the veins of the long neglected Baroque repertoire.

The purists were shocked by Leppard's treatment of Monteverdi's work, claiming that it was a distortion of the composer's music: thickly over-orchestrated and stylistically a travesty. Leppard was quick to point out that there was no definitively correct way to perform this early Italian repertory, for which the composer provided only the bass and the vocal lines leaving the performers to a 'jam-session' in respect of the rest. The composers of the 17th century therefore gave full rein to most of the orchestra, the size of which was unscripted. Leppard argued that if so much leeway had been given to the original performers and they had had access to the number and variety of instrumentalists now available they would have broken loose from the shackles which the purists now enforce in the name of authenticity. Leppard's approach to the performance of this repertoire may have been a step too far, but he has unquestionably been at the forefront of its revitalisation – and I am proud that Glyndebourne played an important part in this story.

In his next steps at Glyndebourne Peter Hall staged the three Mozart/da Ponte operas (*Le nozze di Figaro* in 1973, *Don Giovanni* in 1977 and *Così fan tutte* in 1978) for which he was showered with encomia. Mozart was very much recognised as Glyndebourne's 'house composer', so to find someone so intelligently intrigued with the works of this genius composer was truly a blessing. Hall delved deep into the original texts of da Ponte and succumbed totally to the magical interpretation, drama and entertainment which Mozart brought to them. The results of Hall's trilogy were definitive. (I haven't seen a *Don Giovanni* since which matches his 1977 production – rather like the yard-stick which Busch laid down in his pre-war recording of Glyndebourne's *Don*.)

Hall then directed a couple of Britten's operas – *A Midsummer Night's Dream* (1981), designed by John

Bury, and *Albert Herring* (1985), designed by John Gunter, another of his regular collaborators – which captivated the audience and critics alike, and which brought a truce to 40 years of cold war with Aldeburgh. Peter Pears at the end of the first night of the *Dream* said very simply 'If only Ben could have been here this evening'. *Albert Herring* was an equal success. We eventually sold the production to San Francisco for £75,000, when it looked as if John Graham-Hall was growing out of the central role and I couldn't imagine the production being revived with anyone else. Some years later we took the plunge and bought the production back for £25,000, with Alfie Boe proving that there were other Alberts in the world.

Peter Hall over some 30-odd years directed 19 operas at Glyndebourne – some of the best work of his extensive and remarkable output in the theatre.

I was staying in Aldeburgh sometime in the mid-1990s and visited the librettist Eric Crozier and his wife Nancy for whom her eponymous role in *Herring* was written. Eric told me that he had scripted a scenario for a sequel to this opera and had tried in vain to persuade Britten to turn it into an opera. The proposed sequel starts with Albert Herring travelling to Great Yarmouth where he seeks employment and to escape the burghers of Aldeburgh. In Great Yarmouth he becomes the odd-job man at a B&B, where one day the wife of the B&B's owner tells him to take a cup of tea up to her husband.

Albert does this, only to find the owner *in flagrante delicto*, so leaves the cup of tea as tactfully as he can on a side table. Half an hour later the owner meets up with Albert and hands him a fiver, saying 'There's a good lad'. Albert responds: 'No, £50' – the start of his nefarious career. What a missed opportunity.

In 1972 Bernard Haitink was invited (largely at Dickie's instigation) to conduct *Entführung*. He was at the time the LPO's Chief Conductor. As the LPO was Glyndebourne's orchestra, there was abundant synergy involved in this. Haitink had previously only conducted two operas and was, I think, fascinated by the dramatic dimension that opera would add to his symphonic work. In 1977 Pritchard gave up his position as Glyndebourne's Chief Conductor and Haitink was appointed as his successor – and, at the same time, Pritchard succeeded Haitink as the Chief Conductor for the London Philharmonic Orchestra: perfect symmetry in the play of musical chairs. The combination of Haitink and Hall at the summit of their powers was perhaps reminiscent of the Busch/Ebert era.

During his years at Glyndebourne Haitink conducted 20 operas. It was, I felt, a marriage of kindred spirits. Haitink needed guidance and support in the 'strange world of opera'. He was of course completely at home with mainstream works, but in *Albert Herring* and (I believe) Prokofiev's *The Love for Three Oranges*, he needed familiarisation. In the 1970s he conducted the EMI studio recordings of Glyndebourne's take on the three Mozart/da Ponte operas sponsored by Vincent Meyer (a devoted supporter of Glyndebourne and the LPO). Again, reminiscent of Busch and his acclaimed recordings before the war.

Haitink's years at Glyndebourne were, I believe, not stressful for him. He did not have to fight his or the company's corner with the politicians, or to battle with wanton directors, except in the case of a dreadful production of *Pelléas et Mélisande* in 1976. We felt very much at home with each other – and with Haitink on the podium we knew we had struck gold.

Andrew Davis then took up the baton for some 11 years. In 1973, aged 27, he had taken over *Capriccio* in mid-run from Pritchard and then conducted a kedgeree of operas. He was at the time a man of all trades in his developing command of the repertory. He made the best of a botched production and he brought a good production onto a higher level. Like Haitink, he was a team player – not a characteristic one always associates with principal conductors – in whom egotism seems to be virtually contagious. He conducted with his head and heart in expressive balance. During his tenure as Music Director at Glyndebourne (1989-2000) Davis was appointed Chief Conductor of the BBC

Symphony Orchestra. So his diary was very much filled up with work in the UK until in 2000 Chicago offered him the position of Chief Conductor at the Lyric Opera.

At the end of the 1980s Dickie left Glyndebourne after seven years as General Administrator. He went to Toronto to manage Canada's leading opera company which, like Glyndebourne, was seriously toying with the idea of building a new opera house. Anthony Whitworth-Jones, who qualified as a chartered accountant and very quickly transferred his allegiance to music, became the administrator of the London Sinfonietta, and he then took another leap and followed in Dickie's footsteps as the Administrator of GTO and, subsequently, General Administrator of Glyndebourne. Whitworth-Jones was the fourth chief executive and the third consecutive in-house appointment in Glyndebourne's history to this pivotal position.

Whitworth-Jones liked to challenge his audience. Hence his introduction of new and commissioned operas and some testing productions – starting off with Nigel Osborne's *The Electrification of the Soviet Union* directed by Peter Sellars, a pretty forbidding combination, and continuing with a couple of Harrison Birtwistle operas and Graham Vick's (Glyndebourne's Director of Productions at the time) wrong-headed productions of the Mozart/da Ponte trilogy. (Mind you Vick's other productions at Glyndebourne were straight out of the top drawer. Tchaikovsky's *The Queen of Spades* and *Eugene Onegin*, Rossini's *Ermione* and Debussy's *Pelléas et Mélisande* spring to mind.) It is huge credit to Glyndebourne's audiences that they weathered these artistic storms – and, I suppose, credit to Glyndebourne for cultivating such resilient audiences. In the midst of these challenges there was one opera – very much Whitworth-Jones's choice – *Theodora*, which was given the full treatment of a Peter Sellars 'concept' production and held the audience in thrall. William Christie (no relation but known by my family as 'Cousin Bill') should, as the conductor, take much credit for this thrall too. It also introduced Glyndebourne's rather hesitant courtship with Handel. (*Jephtha* was staged disgracefully in 1966 and is best forgotten.) Leppard and I tried about 20 years ago to persuade Peter Hall to look seriously at some of Handel's massive output, but he was nonplussed by the convention of the *da capos*. Should the singer have made his/her point once, how could he, Hall, keep the dramatic flow going if the point had to be made again. It is only in recent years that directors have got an imaginative grip on this problem: Jean-Marie Villégier in *Rodelinda* and David McVicar in *Giulio Cesare* are good examples. Bill Christie is an important part of Glyndebourne's artistic fabric, and although he has held no overarching position with the company, he has brought into vibrant play the Baroque works (starting with *Theodora*) and pumped a very rewarding asset into Glyndebourne. Handel can provide a limitless source of repertory and I can't understand why we ignore *Tamerlano*. Leppard's recovery of the early Italian operas cannot of course be overshadowed.

So Glyndebourne went through its Mozart, Rossini, the Baroque, Strauss and Janáček decades and Whitworth-Jones added controversially contemporary opera to the brew. The new opera house allowed us to dip our toe into the operas of Wagner, the long held dream of my father whose original plan was to stage Wagner at the first Festival in 1934. Lehnhoff's widely hailed productions of Janáček's three masterpieces, *Kát'a Kabanová, Jenůfa* and *The Makropulos Case*, were crowned by his production of *Tristan und Isolde* with Nina Stemme performing her first major Wagner role and Jiří Bělohlávek conducting. Bělohlávek painstakingly cleared out the accretions of years of invasive tinkering with the score with the result that it sounded joyously almost like chamber music. My father would have been in Nirvana at Glyndebourne's first bold step into the world of Wagner.

An opera house is as good as its spirit of innovation and its quest for discovery or rediscovery, be it of new or neglected works, of talented singers, conductors, directors and designers. It seems to me that as an artistic imperative Glyndebourne should for a definable rolling period champion some particular aspect of the repertoire; should have some recognisable policy which, more than anything by innovation, injects a lively and influential boost to its output.

# ESSENTIAL INGREDIENTS

Glyndebourne's financial stability in the 1960s became shaky on account of weak leadership – so much so that the company in 1966 decided to reduce its output from six productions to four each season. This, of course, attracted a lot of comment in the press and predictions that Glyndebourne was on the brink of collapse. At the same time the Royal Philharmonic Orchestra, Glyndebourne's resident orchestra, was falling apart. The decision was then taken to replace the orchestra with the London Philharmonic Orchestra, which entailed a great deal of delicate negotiation with the outgoing orchestra.

With uplift in Glyndebourne's artistic fortunes at the outset of the 1970s we looked as if we could face the future with optimism, but financial recovery has its own momentum and it was not until the late 1970s that stabilisation was achieved. In 1975 we had a season which included Jonathan Miller's enchanting take on Janáček's *The Cunning Little Vixen* and John Cox's triumphant production of *The Rake's Progress*. There was box office resistance to these operas, so we tried to sell two tickets for the price of one. This confirmed to the press that Glyndebourne's days were truly numbered. However, I had chanced on the answer to a prayer in the shape of an extraordinary individual, Alex Alexander, a Czech by birth who had arrived in the UK shortly before the war to study medicine.

His business career began in Norfolk where he had struck up a friendship with Jack Petre at Westwick Hall. They started to grow fruit and vegetables and set up a plant to freeze these products. He was then approached by Carl Ross, a neighbour, with the proposition that they amalgamate as Ross was freezing fish. Hence the Ross Group which then got hitched up with Imperial Food and became a 'multinational'. I persuaded Alex to support our touring operation and, because of his helpful response, asked him to a Festival performance, which was our first meeting. We had our diaries out before the performance had even started and we became close friends. As a result I asked him to become a Glyndebourne trustee from which position he set about raising the level of sponsorship ten-fold. He also had a material effect on the general perspective of our financial management, and he carried out root and branch changes to our catering contract. All of this rejuvenated Glyndebourne, created vigour and opened up new horizons. He gave us 11 years of his life as a trustee and was then snapped up by the Royal Opera House, where he likewise set about transforming their finances. My father was rescued by Miki Sekers and I by Alex Alexander – both hard-hitting Eastern Europeans.

The trustees at that time were chaired by Sir Anthony Lloyd (later Lord Lloyd of Berwick). Lloyd succeeded Gerald Coke who for 20 years had been more or less the founder Chairman. Coke was an aristocrat and a pre-eminent captain of industry who committed himself to Glyndebourne's welfare. Lloyd did competitively likewise. We had a real sense of comfort generated by the wisdom of these two chairmen, enforced by Peter Baring who succeeded Lloyd and brought a level head and well-balanced judgement to his term of office. The fourth Chairman, John Botts, has reigned almost as long as Coke. He continues to reign – thank heavens. He invited Alexander and me to a very swish lunch at Mark's Club in Mayfair. He was at that time one of Citibank's stars and Alexander targeted him as a potential sponsor. At the end of lunch Botts asked what operas were lined up for the future and I outlined our most immediate plans, mentioning a new production of Bizet's *Carmen* with Haitink conducting and Peter Hall directing his wife Maria Ewing in the title role. Botts looked interested and then said: 'What about the following year?' I told him that we were taking a bit of a leap and would be staging *Porgy and Bess*. He pounced on this with relish (he's American). I told him *Porgy and Bess* was not on offer until we had secured sponsorship for *Carmen*. Botts expressed interest in both operas and asked how much for each. I gave him a figure for *Carmen* (Alexander got nervous) and then a fairly large figure for *Porgy*, which made Alexander's complexion even more pallid. Botts said 'Done' and, being our host at his luncheon club, paid of course for the lunch too.

Botts's very active dedication to the welfare of Glyndebourne became immediately apparent and he was invited to become a trustee of the Glyndebourne Arts Trust, which he accepted – and of which he subsequently became Chairman in 1997. He also joined the Board of Glyndebourne Productions. He has had untold and extraordinary influence on these two bodies, guiding both of them on the straight and creative path to enlightened financial management. Most of the board of directors of Glyndebourne Productions and of the Glyndebourne Arts Trust are now his nominees. I have never known a more generously selfless man.

I want to make one small comment here in contrast to the foregoing comments about the leading lights of Glyndebourne's controlling bodies. All company boards should have a director or whatever who personifies continuity and has a constructive relationship with the chairman. My father had an old family friend, Rhona Byron, on the board of Glyndebourne Productions, who I inherited on my father's death. I, in turn, had Gillian Fane as a member of the board on whom I could lean, who didn't contribute much to boardroom discussions but whose wise and very well informed counsel was comforting, sometimes critical and, more than anything, she was steeped in the history of the place. A person of this disposition helps to bring reality and balance.

Governing boards of charitable organisations tend to be regarded dismissively. For me they bring to the table clarity about the objectives and wellbeing of the company and are owed a debt of gratitude, given that those who sit on them are unpaid, and are often pre-eminent in the rough and tumble of the real world. (Glyndebourne for example had three consecutive Governors of the Bank of England on the Glyndebourne Arts Trust – Leslie O'Brien, Gordon Richardson and Robin Leigh-Pemberton – which must have been reassuring to potential donors.) This also applies to the executive board of Glyndebourne Productions (also a charity), who have considerably more substantive responsibilities. On the grounds of manageability and effectiveness I never allowed Glyndebourne Productions to have more than six directors, as against 15 or more people on the Trust, the chairman of which has tended to be a member of the executive board. This ensured to a degree that the left hand of governance knew what the right hand was up to.

An indispensable ingredient in Glyndebourne's output is its orchestras. Because they play in the pit rather than on a concert hall platform they tend to be taken by a lot of the audience for granted. Before the war Glyndebourne engaged a 'scratch' orchestra, the London Symphony Orchestra in disguise, containing some of the cream of Britain's great instrumentalists (such as the oboist Evelyn Rothwell – later Lady Barbirolli). In 1948 Beecham's Royal Philharmonic Orchestra then became Glyndebourne's 'house orchestra' – as good an orchestra as you could get, but in 1963 disintegration set in as some of its key players defected and found refuge and far more financial security in the BBC Symphony Orchestra. The London Philharmonic Orchestra has ever since been an answer to Glyndebourne's prayers. It has had its troughs but its peaks have been extensively more prominent. A new management was brought in under the very capable leadership of Serge Dorny in 1996, a position he held until 2003. Dorny in the course of time transferred his allegiance to Opéra de Lyon, where he has received international recognition for his imaginative artistry and financial grasp. He witnessed the very delicate process of reducing the

LPO's orchestral monopoly at Glyndebourne to provide space for the advent of a second orchestra, the Orchestra of the Age of Enlightenment. Dickie must be given considerable credit for the introduction of the OAE at Glyndebourne. He attended a concert conducted by Simon Rattle and was quick to recognise that period instruments were an irresistible way forward in the performance of Baroque music, and in the course of time other music composed for these instruments. There is now a regular pattern with the LPO performing in four productions in each Festival and the OAE in two. It seems to be a workable pattern. Glyndebourne is fortunate beyond measure to have two such outstanding orchestras. They are carat jewels in Glyndebourne's crown. Incidentally, David Pickard, the OAE's Chief Executive (1993-2001) became Glyndebourne's sixth General Director in 2001. The LPO, particularly under Vladimir Jurowski's leadership (he was appointed as Glyndebourne's Music Director in 2001 and the LPO's Principal Guest Conductor in 2003) competes with any international orchestra. Jurowski has brought to it a distinctive style through the power of his intellect, his emotional resource and real discipline. And, by the way, his LPO programming for the concert platform has been truly innovative.

Notable in the brief tenure of Nicholas Snowman as General Director (1998-2000) was the appointment of Jurowski and the engagement of David McVicar. It should be said that McVicar, who holds no overarching position like the principal directors who I have so far referred to, has had material effect on Glyndebourne. He is one of the few directors around who is prepared to risk his neck on directing repertory which challenges the yard stick of judgement created over years of repeated performances. His deft touch of marrying tradition with modernity has resulted in productions of remarkable clarity. His *Cesare*, in particular, was an overwhelming success.

Singers are judged without recourse to any defence once they get to an opening night – a daunting moment. They are of course in the thrall of the conductor and director, whilst at the same time expected to bring into play their own feelings about, and interpretation of, the role. There is little that disturbs me more than casting an opera without the close involvement of the conductor and director, who are essential to the homogeneity of the whole process. So the singers are naturally in the front line and are frequently the element in a production by which it is remembered.

When staging an opera Glyndebourne has never sought to give priority to star singers. It can't afford to. It is an ensemble house, but nevertheless it has attracted a great many singers on the edge of 'stardom'. In addition to those already mentioned there is a multitude of singers who laid claim to stardom; to list them would be a chapter in itself.

Another indispensable ingredient is, of course, the music staff, made up of a group of very fine pianists who accompany the rehearsals assiduously before the onslaught of the orchestra, and coach the singers intensively, both principals and understudies in their roles. Jani Strasser was head of the music staff for many years and made sure that everyone knew this. Martin Isepp who had been on the music staff since 1958 eventually succeeded him in 1975 – another in-house appointment which has been a bit of a trade mark at Glyndebourne. Administration was not Martin's strong point, but he made up for this by his fine musicianship (he was an internationally acclaimed accompanist). In 1998 Steven Naylor, a repetiteur for some years, assumed control of this department with administrative flair and continues to do so. By the time of the orchestra's arrival the casts of the operas and the chorus are well-prepared and in very performable shape.

Glyndebourne has always aimed to be self-sufficient. We have always run our own wardrobe, props and wigs departments – and in the old days we built our scenery, but in time found that outsourcing this work was more effective and cheaper. The skilled output of these departments is under the management of the technical director who has responsibility for all the backstage staff and stage management. The technical director must ensure that rehearsals and performances run without a hitch, embracing a wide diversity of fundamentally important and interlinked functions. Glyndebourne has always had the good fortune to be served by highly competent technical directors, not least by its most recent incumbent, Dave Locker. Directors new to Glyndebourne are invariably *bouleversés* by the assiduous and creative care they receive from this enabling team.

The ushers – with whom the audience has closest contact – are extolled too. There was an occasion years ago when at the end of a performance a rumpus occurred with one member of the audience accusing another of walking off with her mink stole. An usher intervened in the squabble and asked the accused 'felon' to hand over the stole, sniffed it and then, having sniffed the two ladies reached his verdict and restored the stolen stole to its rightful owner. Good presence of mind.

An unavoidable and treasured ingredient in Glyndebourne is its topography – its location and the care and cultivation devoted to it. The gardens are effectively foyers – Elysian on a fine evening and (need I say it) miserable on a wet and windy one – with the stunning backdrop of the South Downs, now given the status of a National Park. This formalisation of the status of the Downs rankles a touch with me. The Downs have an umbilical cord to the infinite past, but the present day legislators pay no heed to the cause for the natural preservation of this land, preservation which is totally accountable over centuries to the landowners. Those now entrusted with the conservation of the Downs have wide–ranging powers to exercise control over and administer the use of the land and have, to all appearances, assumed virtual ownership, whilst in actual fact the land remains in the ownership of its centuries-old custodians. As it turns out, to date, the recently introduced classification of the Downs appears to have made little difference. (Access to the public and right to roam has never been a problem.) However, it would be reassuring if there was a bit more recognition of the part played by the landowners. There – I've got that off my chest.

Apart from the coastline, the Downs remain unafflicted by development of any major dimension. Glyndebourne could, I suppose, be accounted as a small blot on the landscape, but is tucked into a valley unseen from any surrounding thoroughfare. Incidentally I don't find it a blot. The gardens are a natural out-growth and progression from their surroundings – and integral to the Glyndebourne experience. When my father inherited the property at the end of the First World War he made some significant changes, extending the lawns and landscaping the ponds. When my wife, Mary, came on the scene she made many (but not fundamental) changes. She had the misfortune to have a series of unsympathetic head-gardeners, but having weathered this storm she landed up in clover with two consecutive head-gardeners who really knew their onions, Chris Hughes and then Kevin Martin – who came up through the ranks and now leads the team. She also had the particularly good fortune to team up with Christopher Lloyd, her gardening guru, who out of unpaid love advised her on countless aspects of the garden. When he effectively retired from his unpaid position he was succeeded by Lady Mary Keen (also unpaid) whose input in making some inevitably very necessary changes to the gardens during the rebuild were vital. Mary Keen, very bossy by nature, told me one day when we were close to completion of the new building to regard the gardens as having as much priority as the building. Advice which I have heeded. Mary, my wife, has in very large measure been the guiding inspiration for the garden's development and changes over 45 years. We now have a treasurable guru, John Hoyland, who is holding the whole thing together in the ever-changing world of gardening. Horticulture and opera are, I frequently feel, comfortable companions. I believe much of the audience share this viewpoint.

# GLYNDEBOURNE'S REBIRTH

From the early 1960s I became increasingly concerned about the inadequacy of Glyndebourne's ageing and makeshift theatre which had grown from 300 seats in 1934 to 762 at the time of my father's death – he adored tinkering with the place.

I bided my time.

In 1986 I saw the country's prospect of financial growth set fair and my first hint of an intention to tackle Glyndebourne's problems was touched upon in my foreword to the 1986 Programme Book. I got no feedback to this, and even my governing boards paid scant attention to my opinion. I had an abiding love for the old building, but this was outweighed by my concern for its future and the competition it would inevitably face. I gave myself two years to find an architect, two years to raise the finance and select a team, and two years to build. Things started to get serious with the selection of the architects, Michael and Patty

Hopkins, and Stuart Lipton of Stanhope Properties provided invaluable advice lining up a first-class team of consultants. John Bury (Peter Hall's principal set designer) was chosen as adviser on all theatrical matters and there was no better man for the job.

The fundraising strategy was devised simply but effectively by Mark Beddy, Glyndebourne's Finance Director. He was a man of formidable intellect, a colleague indispensable to me, and someone who I trusted. He also, perhaps unusually for a chartered accountant, possessed a total grasp of man-management, commanding universal respect from the entire workforce, and of course from all heads of department and those entrusted with ultimate control. In short, a treasure.

John Botts assumed a role which encompassed every aspect of the building process, from fundraising to the appointment of hard-hitting board members and the selection of advisers. His unswerving dedication, enthusiasm and constructive input in the rebuild and in its subsequent operation are matched by nobody in Glyndebourne's history.

It was fun opening the post. I never had any sleepless nights over raising the money. We started with a blitz on our corporate supporters who responded with extraordinary alacrity and generosity. By early 1992 we had reached 80 per cent of our £33 million target and found ourselves in competition with Compton Verney's proposed new opera house in the Midlands and their powerful executive.

We grasped the initiative and I persuaded my Board to go for it. Bovis were chosen as the building contractors who were headed by their very experienced and enthusiastic Construction Manager, Alan Lansdell. He was key in keeping the schedule and budget on track, a particular challenge given the complexity of the contract. Compton Verney retreated leaving us with an open market-place. Our Project Manager, Eric Gabriel, representing Glyndebourne's interests, was already in place. Eric was recommended to me by Jacob Rothschild, Chairman of the National Gallery which was in the process of completing the building of the Sainsbury Wing, project managed by Gabriel. I invited Eric down to Glyndebourne to discuss his participation as a contract manager. Anthony Whitworth-Jones attended the meeting and witnessed the discussion between Gabriel and me where neither of us gave an inch – like two dogs with a bone. Anthony said to me 'Well he certainly hasn't got the job', to which I replied 'He most certainly has'. I have never met such a safe pair of hands. Eric's grasp of detail, his long and all-embracing experience of the building trade and his unbounded enthusiasm for the rebuild brought the whole thing to reality – on schedule and on budget.

Our tails have wagged vigorously ever since. You can't have a better friend.

We built the new Peter Hall rehearsal stage before the opening of the Festival in 1992. We cordoned it off, and in the process showed our audience life was getting rather serious as far as the rebuild was concerned. This was a healthy development, particularly because we looked serious in our intent and invaluable support came in as a result. The shortened Festival in 1992 weathered the proximity of its new neighbour under the generous tolerance of a sympathetically-disposed audience.

A fundraising Gala in the presence of Prince Charles was held at the end of the Festival with the conductors Davis and Haitink, and the singers Frederica von Stade, Monserrat Caballé, Ruggero Raimondi, Felicity Lott, Benjamin Luxon, Cynthia Haymon and Kim Begley together with the London Philharmonic Orchestra and the Glyndebourne Chorus. All gave their services for free. The caterers did likewise, and the champagne and fine wine was donated by the growers. The auditorium and marquee (which had been put up in the field next to the ha-ha) were packed and the BBC filmed the whole event which I compered, with added tributes from Janet Baker, Geraint Evans and Elisabeth Söderström. The evening netted £850,000.

The demolition gang moved in the following week and it took exactly one day to reduce the auditorium and its front of house to rubble. The fly tower was a more complex problem and a crane of substantial proportions was brought in and the whole of the fly tower was lifted off in one. There was a point when the crane driver had reached the near maximum capacity and he made as if to move out, but our team held him firmly in place and told him to keep going. He had no alternative but to do so. There was huge jubilation when this large piece of structure hit the ground.

Almost immediately the site was cleared and building work on the new theatre started. The new theatre is designed without any timber or metal support. It is almost throughout dependent on load-bearing brick – a hell of a lot of brick. The people chosen to provide the brick and lay it could not believe their luck. Because we were building in a recession we were able to mop up the best and most skilled brickies in the country – and this state of good fortune extended of course to all the other trades employed on site.

By 1993 the building kept pace with the schedule and kept gratifyingly within budget. Any changes suggested by the architect were kept in very close check, each suggested change incurring needless cost. Gabriel and Lansdell held all this under a very tight rein.

Hopkins on the whole responded to the strict parameters as a result. The only overspend of any significance related to the Peter Hall rehearsal room where Hopkins had designed an external cover of grassland which was totally impractical as far as upkeep was concerned. Six months after the 'bunker' had been in place, Hopkins looked at it in some despair and thought it should be finished in material in which it had been originally designed, much to my glee. It cost a bomb but it works to everyone's satisfaction. In early 1994 there was jubilation when the rebuild reached completion. 'Snagging' then was the main consideration. Remarkably little 'snagging' was needed because of the very efficient management of the development and because the client knew very precisely what he and his colleagues wanted – a characteristic not common to most large developments.

Come March 1994 we mounted a concert at which we tested the acoustics with Andrew Davis and Bernard Haitink conducting the London Philharmonic Orchestra and an impressive line-up of artists. At the end of the concert a number of people came up to me and said 'Isn't it a bit eccentric to have this acoustic test on 28th March in the knowledge you will be opening the new house on

28th May. There will be no opportunity to make any significant changes you might think necessary'. I responded by saying that was precisely the point. I didn't want to make any changes – I knew I would not have to in the knowledge that any changes would be detrimental and would almost certainly result in needless damage to the acoustics and the appearance of the auditorium. It is always necessary when dealing with acoustics that you give a place a chance to bed down and wait for the reaction of your audience, some say three years later, by which time you can get a fully considered response on which you might be persuaded to make changes. Mass view is the right way so don't tinker with the acoustics until that point is reached. Incidentally, we have never tinkered with the acoustics. My brief to the acousticians was for absolute clarity as far as the singers and the orchestra were concerned so all the words and instruments would be clearly heard and, at the same time, I wanted a lot of resonance to flatter the voices and the instruments. Derek Sugden, the acoustician at Arup Acoustics, responded to this by saying I was asking him to meet a couple of incompatibles to which I replied that that was his job. I think he achieved this brief magnificently.

The new theatre opened on 28th May 1994 with *Le nozze di Figaro*, conducted by Haitink, on the same date where 60 years earlier, Busch had conducted the same opera in the original opera house. The first audiences I think came prepared for a bit of a culture shock because, of course, they had lost an old friend with which they had become comfortable, despite its shortcomings, and were not certain how they were going to take to their new one. The most reassuring remark I received from members of the audience on the opening night, and at later performances, was 'Thank God nothing has changed', a pause, 'but for the better'.

I believe my parents would have loved the new theatre, but I think my father would have come up with a different design for the flytower. My mother would, I am sure, simply adore it as it stands.

# A THIRD GENERATION

Anumber of quite major changes took place at Glyndebourne in the last years of the decade, indeed millennium. I officially retired on 31st December 1999 but my wife and I continued to live at Glyndebourne until the end of 2001, and I continued during those two years to retain a position on the Board of Glyndebourne Productions and to have an administrative role during the handover period to my second son, Gus. It was a handover that thankfully worked seamlessly. After Gus left university he started on a career in wildlife, not exactly a choice of profession one might expect the future Chairman of Glyndebourne would embark upon. He adored it, and was successful at it, which gave me the willies, since it looked as if I could be at risk of him being so immersed in wildlife that he might lose interest in inheriting Glyndebourne and the offer of chairmanship. My fears were allayed. He was 36 when I officially retired and I promised I would vacate my occupancy of the house within two years. I couldn't have a better successor. He brings to his job as Chairman a true understanding of modern technology of which he has a complete grasp. He is remarkably good at delegation and there is not much question as to who rules the roost. To have a father, son and now grandson all avidly wedded to the management of a business is a rarity. My father would be thrilled by the achievement and spirit of dedication which Gus is creating.

During the handover period I saw the completion of the last major development of the rebuild, namely the construction of a second rehearsal stage, virtually identical to the first rehearsal space and again equivalent in dimension to our main stage area. I was fortunate in persuading the Jerwood Foundation to finance some 40 per cent of the cost – by far the largest contribution to the rebuild programme. 2002 saw Gus's full accession. He turfed me out of Glyndebourne, and I turfed him out of the nice farmhouse he was occupying.

It felt odd after 67 years for me and 44 years for Mary, but the indulgence of irresponsibility has (at least for me) taken a bit of a grip. Mary has given me uplift for the last 56 years. She has provided me with support at Glyndebourne which has surpassed what I could conceivably have looked for. She has brought an essential ingredient to Glyndebourne, as my mother did, namely a strong and all-pervasive heart to the place. Without the guidance she has given me, Glyndebourne would not be the place it now is.

I look back over the last 80 years with a sense of pride and gratitude for what my parents created, for the enormous contribution made by all those who have participated in this journey of endeavour, but above all for the heartbeat which is the core of Glyndebourne's existence and for which I hold my wife, Mary, responsible.

*Adieu my beloved Glyndebourne*

# Illustrations

**Page 4:**
*George Christie, 1960.*
photo: Guy Gravett

**Page 9:**
*Louise Christie, aged eight, with her father, George Christie.*
photo: Guy Gravett

**Page 33:**
*(top) The Christie family 1937. John Christie and Audrey Mildmay, with toddler George and his big sister Rosamond.*
photo: Bassano
*(bottom) Glyndebourne: the house, organ room and theatre. The latter is partially hidden by the new block containing dressing rooms and the artist's green room, 1936.*
photo: The Glyndebourne Archive

**Page 34:**
*(top) Carl Ebert: Artistic Director 1934-1959.*
photo: Guy Gravett
*(bottom) Fritz Busch, Music Director, in conversation with Rudolf Bing, General Manager, 1936.*
photo: The Glyndebourne Archive

**Page 35:**
*(top) Moran Caplat: General Manager 1949-1981.*
photo: Guy Gravett
*(bottom left) Sock the pug dog, who in later life was always held to run Glyndebourne – by John Christie at least.*
photo: Guy Gravett
*(bottom right) Jani Strasser: Head of Music Staff 1934-1970.*
photo: Guy Gravett

**Page 36:**

*(top left) George Christie as Fleance with Owen Brannigan in the 1947 revival of* Macbeth – *one of the two operas mounted by Glyndebourne at the Festival it co-founded in Edinburgh.*
photo: Angus McBean

*(top right) Miki Sekers: a trustee of the Glyndebourne Arts Trust.*
photo: Guy Gravett

*(bottom) Members of the Festival Society Committee at the House of Lords, 1954. Mr H G Herrington, Mr O B Miller, John Christie, George Christie, Miki Sekers.*
photo: Guy Gravett


**Page 37:**

*(top) Graziella Sciutti as Rosina with Oliver Messel on the set he designed for* Il barbiere di Siviglia, *1954.*
photo: Guy Gravett

*(bottom) Vittorio Gui: Artistic Counsellor. Head of Music 1960-1963.*
photo: Guy Gravett


**Page 38:**

*(top left) John Pritchard: Music Director 1963-1977.*
photo: Guy Gravett

*(top right) Günther Rennert: Artistic Counsellor. Head of Production 1960-1967.*
photo: Guy Gravett

*(bottom) Régine Crespin (the Marschallin) and Elisabeth Söderström (Octavian) in Strauss's* Der Rosenkavalier, *1959.*
photo: Guy Gravett


**Page 39:**

*(top left) Director Franco Enriquez and designer Emanuele Luzzati on the set of* Die Entführung aus dem Serail, *1968.*
photo: Guy Gravett

*(top right) Designer David Hockney and producer John Cox on the set of their famous production* The Rake's Progress, *1975.*
photo: Guy Gravett

*(bottom) Ptolemy (Tol) Christie's christening:1971. George Christie cutting the cake watched by Mary Christie, Gus Christie and conductor Raymond Leppard, Tol's godfather.*
photo: Guy Gravett

**Page 40:**

*(top) The Glyndebourne Arts trustees and friends on the terrace in 1983: Sir Anthony Lloyd, John Barden, Leopold de Rothschild, Sir Alex Alexander, n/k, Mary Christie, Lady Rupert Neville, n/k, Hon Mrs Cazalet, Robin Leigh-Pemberton, The Lord Briggs, Sir Emmanuel Kaye, Brian Nicholson, Moran Caplat.*
photo: Guy Gravett
*(bottom) Members of the Glyndebourne Productions board in 1960: Lt Col CHN Adams, E Scott Norman, Janet Moores (Secretary), George Christie (Chairman), Moran Caplat, Rhona Byron, Gerald Coke, John Christie.*
photo: Guy Gravett

**Page 41:**

*(top left) Peter Hall: Artistic Director 1984-1990.*
photo: Guy Gravett
*(top right) Brian Dickie: General Administrator 1982-1988.*
photo: Guy Gravett
*(bottom) Bernard Haitink: Music Director 1978-1988.*
photo: Guy Gravett

**Page 42:**

*(top) The curtain call at the fundraising Gala, 1992. Ruggero Raimondi, Cynthia Haymon, Andrew Davis, Monserrat Caballé, George Christie, Felicity Lott, Bernard Haitink, Frederica von Stade, Benjamin Luxon, Janet Baker, Kim Begley.*
photo: Guy Gravett
*(bottom) Architect Michael Hopkins, George Christie and designer/theatre consultant, John Bury, 1991.*
photo: Richard Davies

**Page 43:**

*(top) Removal of the old fly tower steelwork, 1992.*
photo: Joanna Townsend
*(bottom left) Acoustician Derek Sugden firing a starting pistol from the stage to test the acoustics in the new theatre, 1993.*
photo: Guy Gravett
*(bottom right) Topping off the new roof, 1993.*
photo: Gus Christie

**Page 44:**
*(top) Anthony Whitworth-Jones: General Director 1989-1998.*
photo: Guy Gravett
*(bottom) Graham Vick and Andrew Davies in rehearsal for* Lulu,
*1996.*
photo: Mike Hoban

**Page 45:**
*(top) The 1994 gardening team: Chris Hughes, Mary Christie,*
*Kevin Martin, Graham Harvey, Giles Parker.*
photo: Guy Gravett
*(bottom left) Family friend, and board stalwart, Gillian Fane with*
*her Scottie dog Jock, 1982.*
photo: Guy Gravett
*(bottom right) Finance Director Mark Beddy.*
photo: Gus Christie

**Page 46:**
*(top) The new opera house nestled in the Downs.*
photo: Mike Hoban
*(bottom) The auditorium of the new theatre.*
photo: Mike Hoban

**Page 47:**
*Three generations of Glyndebourne Christies: Gus Christie and*
*George Christie in front of the Oscar Nemon bust of John Christie,*
*1999.*
photo: Mike Hoban

**Page 48:**
*Members of the audience enjoying Glyndebourne's 'bucolic setting',*
*1963.*
photo: Guy Gravett

**Page 87:**
*Mary Christie, 1960.*
photo: Guy Gravett

# Timeline

**1931**
- Marriage of John Christie and Audrey Mildmay

**1934**
- First Glyndebourne Festival
- Fritz Busch appointed Music Director, GFO (until 1951)
- Carl Ebert appointed Artistic Director, GFO (until 1959)
- Jani Strasser appointed Head of Music Staff, GFO (until 1970)

**1936**
- Rudolf Bing appointed General Manager, GFO (until 1949)

**1939**
- Formation of Glyndebourne Productions Limited (GPL)

**1947**
- First Edinburgh Festival

**1949**
- Moran Caplat appointed General Manager, GFO (until 1981)

**1951**
- Death of Fritz Busch

**1953**
- Death of Audrey Mildmay

**1954**
- Formation of Glyndebourne Arts Trust (GAT)
- Miki Sekers appointed a trustee of GAT (until 1972)

**1958**
- Marriage of George Christie and Mary Nicholson

**1959**
- Retirement of Carl Ebert

**1960**
- Günther Rennert appointed Artistic Director, GFO (until 1967)
- Vittorio Gui appointed Artistic Counsellor and Head of Music, GFO (until 1963)

**1961**
- Birth of Hector Thomas Cleveland Christie

**1962**
- Death of John Christie

**1963**
- Birth of Augustus (Gus) Jack Christie
- John Pritchard appointed Music Director, GFO (until 1977)

**1964**
- London Philharmonic Orchestra, first season as Resident Orchestra

**1966**
- Birth of Patricia Louise Christie

**1967**
- Gillian Fane appointed a director of GPL (until 1999)

**1968**
- Glyndebourne Touring Opera (GTO) makes its inaugural tour
- Brian Dickie appointed Administrator, GTO (until 1981)

**1972**
- John Cox appointed Artistic Director, GFO (until 1981)

**1974**
- Birth of Ivor Ptolemy (Tol) Christie

**1975**
- Martin Isepp appointed Head of Music Staff (until 1993)

**1976**
- Alex Alexander appointed a trustee of GAT (until 1987)

**1978**
- Bernard Haitink appointed Music Director, GFO (until 1988)

**1981**
- Anthony Whitworth-Jones appointed Administrator, GTO (until 1988)
- Alex Alexander appointed a director of GPL (until 1989)

**1982**
- Brian Dickie appointed General Administrator, GFO (until 1988)

**1984**
- Glyndebourne Festival Opera's 50th anniversary
- Peter Hall appointed Artistic Director, GFO (until 1990)

**1987**
- John Botts appointed a trustee of GAT, appointed Chairman in 1997 (until 2014)

**1988**
- Mark Beddy appointed Financial and Commercial Director (until 1997)

**1989**
- Anthony Whitworth-Jones appointed General Director, GFO (until 1998)
- Andrew Davis appointed Music Director, GFO (until 2000)
- John Botts joined the GPL board, appointed Chairman in 2015
- Orchestra of the Age of Enlightenment (OAE), first season

**1992**
- Last season in old theatre

**1993**
- Graham Vick appointed Director of Productions, GFO (until 2000)

**1994**
- Opening of new opera house

**1998**
- Nicholas Snowman appointed General Director, GFO (until 2000)

**1999**
- Retirement of George Christie as Chairman of Glyndebourne

**2000**
- Gus Christie appointed Executive Chairman of Glyndebourne

**2001**
- David Pickard appointed General Director, GFO (until 2015)
- Vladimir Jurowski appointed Music Director, GFO (until 2013)

**2002**
- OAE made Associate Orchestra

key

GFO Glyndebourne Festival Opera
GTO Glyndebourne Touring Opera
GPL Glyndebourne Productions Limited
GAT Glyndebourne Arts Trust

# Sir George Christie, CH
## 31st December 1934 – 7th May 2014

George Christie took over from his father to become Chairman of Glyndebourne Productions Limited in 1958. During his tenure as Chairman he served on many artistic boards, including the Gulbenkian Foundation, Arts Council England, the London Philharmonic Orchestra and the London Sinfonietta. Among his many achievements at Glyndebourne, he was most notably responsible for the founding of Glyndebourne Touring Opera in 1968 and the rebuilding of the new opera house which opened in 1994. He held several honorary degrees, and was appointed Cavaliere al Merito della Repubblica Italiana in 1977, and, in France, Commandeur, l'Ordre des Arts et des Lettres in 2006. Sir George was knighted in 1984 for his services to music and made a Companion of Honour in 2001.

*A Slim Volume*
*Glyndebourne: an anecdotal account*
by George Christie

Published by Glyndebourne Productions Limited
© George Christie/Glyndebourne Productions Limited

First published in May 2016

The final chapter in *A Slim Volume* contains brief excerpts of George Christie's text from *Glyndebourne: A Visual History*, published in 2009 by Glyndebourne Productions Limited.

Edited by Joanna Townsend with grateful thanks to Karen Anderson, Julia Aries and Joyce Kennedy
Designed by Valerie Sargent
Printed in England at Pureprint Group, Uckfield, East Sussex

Glyndebourne
Lewes BN8 5UU
+44 (0) 1273 812 321

glyndebourne.com

Glyndebourne Productions Limited
Registered No 358266 England
Glyndebourne is a registered charity
Charity No 243877

ISBN 978-0-9538749-9-6

9 780953 874996 >